# Never Forget

## who the F*ck you are

Reflections Journal
by

# ANQUESHA TILLMAN

Book cover design: *Gram Telen*
Book format: *Gram Telen*
Book inspiration: *Anquesha Tillman*
Illustrations: *Antaripa Tamuli*
Editor: *Kalenthia Hobbs Sims*

I dedicate this reflection journal to my amazing children, Juquan, Jaiden, and Kourtnie. I am beyond blessed and forever grateful to be your mother. You all gave me a newfound love that I never could have imaged. God knew exactly what I needed at the age of 18, 21 and 30. The three of you provide me with more love than anyone could ever ask for in a lifetime. I do not take your love or our relationships for granted, and I am honored that God hand-selected each one of you for me and your fathers. To my mother, Lynette, you are the epitome of everything about love. I love you with every ounce of blood in my body. Thank you for being who you are called to be. You have always allowed me to be me and helped shape me into the person I am today. You give me more support and guidance than I could ever repay. To my grandmothers, Betty and Lucille, I love you both for your journeys, your faith, and your unconditional love. There is nothing in this WORLD better than having two praying grandmothers. To my fathers, Gary and Gregory, each of you play an especially significant role in my life. At the age of forty-one,

I understand why I had this journey with both of you and I appreciate the love, guidance, support, and respect both of you provide to me. To my siblings, Frederick, Mallissa, Joanna, Davarris and Keeyawna, you all know what time it is. We are the true definition of a blended family, and no one could ever tell us anything different. We are family and have been family since day one. I love each of you with everything. It is all the memories, summer vacations, and shenanigans for me. We have an UNBREAKABLE bond. To my besties, my sister-friends and my heartbeats, Jamila, Latoya, and Trameka #GoldenGirlsForever. We have 30 years of an unbreakable friendship with many more years to go. Although I love people, I do not like a ton of people in my space. I am happy we met during my extrovert years! To my amazing aunties, uncles, beautiful nieces, talented nephews, and best cousins ever; I love you all for your strength, your dedication to this family, and all the things that we fight through with GOD first. To my GLBB, Kenneth, thank you for your endless love, your journey, and our future. I love the way you love me even when you do not understand. I cannot wait to see God continue to use you. To my father, GOD, you are my everything. I could not do this without you. I am nothing without you. I am thankful for each day that you continue to include me in the number. Thank you for your Son, the Word, and the Holy Spirit. My soul, spirit, and flesh love you forever!

Rest In Peace my heavenly angels, Eva Mae Shirley *my first Superwoman*, Doris Gilbert, Lillian Dennard, and Crystal Davis.

#Fierce #Strong #Loving
#WomenofGod #UrJourniesWereBeautiful
#ForeverMissed #UrLegaciesWillLiveOn

# Acknowledgement

Thank you, Kalenthia Hobbs Sims, for pouring out your time, attention, excitement, and unwavering love for me. You have walked with me throughout this journey from the first time I reached out to you, until the time I finally said, "I'm ready to publish this reflection journal." You have been my ROCK. I am so thankful to God, that you were such an instrumental part of this process because it was not easy. Your faith in God showed up and your wisdom is pure. I love you!

# Preface

This reflection journal captures many moments that exemplify a few of my life lessons; the painful and powerful growth moments, awareness, and understanding how to love myself while connecting the dots to try and understand my overall purpose. While navigating through life, I have always reflected throughout my journey capturing moments that stood out to me the most. The moments that caught my attention, made me dig a little deeper to find a connection, forced me to answer my why, made me ponder, made me cry, but ultimately brought me so much hope and joy. Reflecting throughout life was therapeutic for my mind, body, and soul. It allowed me to understand the bigger picture of my life. Thus far, I have endured many revelations while in this space. There were many seasons to endure, with many lessons learned. I have always walked away somewhat scared, full, and excited about what was next. While reflecting, I spend most of my time reading the word, sitting on my back deck, praising God, being still, showing gratitude, sitting by the water, taking long walks, or sitting in silence. This is where my magic begins. As I wrote this reflection journal, I had to capture my notes while I was truly in the midst of the experience where my mind, body, and soul were one. This was mystical and unforgettable! The words would just flow from my heart to my notepad and connect organically. Nothing that I have said in this journal is new on earth. Nothing that I have disclosed has not been seen before. I am not writing and sharing this with you to make it seem as if I have found all the answers because honestly friends, *I am laughing on the inside,* I have not. I am sharing my deepest, most intimate moments of my life with you because I was led by God to share them. This is me being obedient. This is my truth and my story. I am not sure who this will help but I am excited for the future because I was led to do this. It was a burning fire that never diminished. This was not a goal of mine... May God bless you throughout this journey.

Remember to Rejoice in our hope. Be patient in trouble, and keep praying... Romans 12:12

Queesh

52 Lists
for
Happiness
NIV
WOMEN'S
Devotional Bible
New International Version
The original collection of daily devotions
from godly women

*A Special Note to my Readers*
*Before you get Started...*

- *While reading this reflection journal, after each pearl take a moment to reflect and jot down your true thoughts & feelings – grab a journal...*

- *Be honest with yourself - this is going to be key to your desired success ...*

- *Be intentional about your growth – this part!*

- *Set or reset your goals as needed - this is your journey; you are the author... draft your book as you see fit...*

- *Always Bet on yourself...*

- *Do not rush the process - enjoy the ride, it will be worth it...*

- *Add a calendar reminder to follow up and review your progress from time to time - this step is just as important as the others to see your growth – you will be proud of yourself ...*

- *Show yourself Grace and Love* ❤

# Pearls

**Navigating Through Life...** ......................**16**

- Chapter One... .....................17
- Yesterday, Today, and Tomorrow... ............19
- Everyday Introduces New Opportunities... .....21
- Foundation... ......................22
- Is Life Unfair... .....................25
- Daily Regulation... ...................27
- Why... ..........................30
- A Sincere Apology to my Mother... ...........32

**Awareness...** .........................**35**

- Crystal Davis... .....................36
- I Love Us... .......................39
- Don't Put Yourself in a Box... ..............43
- Try Not to be Confused... .................45
- Sister, Pastor, Sarah Jakes Roberts... ..........48
- Don't be too Busy... ...................53
- Be Careful not to Succumb to the Noise... .....60

- I Didn't Follow my Own Rules... . . . . . . . . . . . . . .61
- Make Sure You Value Your "No"... . . . . . . . . . .63

**Painful, Powerful Growth Moments… . . . . . . . . . . . 65**
- Gracefully Broken... . . . . . . . . . . . . . . . . . . . .66
- Was I Not Enough... . . . . . . . . . . . . . . . . . . . .69
- The Closet... . . . . . . . . . . . . . . . . . . . . . . . .72
- Feeling Numb... . . . . . . . . . . . . . . . . . . . . . .74
- I'm Good, I'm Ok... . . . . . . . . . . . . . . . . . . . .79
- When I Thought I Couldn't Hear... . . . . . . . . . .81
- Shit Runs Deep... . . . . . . . . . . . . . . . . . . . . .85
- Stand in Your Truth... . . . . . . . . . . . . . . . . . .89
- The Moment I Stopped Feeling Like a Failure... . . . . . . . . . . . . . . . . . . . . . .95
- Apologies, Forgiveness and Being Intentional... . . . . . . . . . . . . . . . . . . . .99
- There's a Difference Between Changing on Your Own or Being Forced... . . . . . . . . . . . .102
- Let Your Guard Down... . . . . . . . . . . . . . . . .106

**Understanding My Purpose and Loving Myself… . 108**
- Defining Success... . . . . . . . . . . . . . . . . . . .109
- Starting Over... . . . . . . . . . . . . . . . . . . . . . .111
- Understanding Your Purpose... . . . . . . . . . . .115
- Trust the Process... . . . . . . . . . . . . . . . . . . .119
- I Dare You to BET on Yourself... . . . . . . . . . . .123
- Ponder on This... . . . . . . . . . . . . . . . . . . . . .125

- Stop Procrastinating............................127
- Selfish or Not... ...........................129
- The Assignment or Not... ...................132
- Dear Me in my 30's.... ......................137
- Never Forget who the F👑ck you are .......140

# Navigating Through Life...

Never Forget Who The F*ck You Are

# Chapter One...

*H*ello friends, my name is Anquesha Tillman, I am still smiling and enjoying life at the age of forty-one and truly learning that 'thy later days, will be my better days.' I am first a child of God, always searching to ensure, while being blessed to see another day that my purpose according to God's will is fulfilled. I understand as my faith gets stronger that I am here to serve, love, and to be kind. I would not have it any other way. I am a loving-faithful daughter, granddaughter, mother, sister, friend, life-partner, aunt, cousin, and the list goes on.

As you embark on this journey with me, take time to reflect, let's show ourselves some grace, give love, go through the seasons man oh man the seasons, and live through the moment for the future. My heart desires to see us prosper and to reach the desires of our spiritual self as it aligns with our purpose. I am a believer and will *always seek God's voice throughout my journey. Please enjoy the ride without placing ourselves in a box. Love, Love, Love!*

*Wishing you much success as we embark on this venture!*

*Queesh*

# Yesterday, Today, and Tomorrow...

*O*hhhmmmmmggggggggggeeeee!! *This is one of the most profound, yet simplest tactic that I love to use to reset myself...*

*I cannot focus on yesterday because it is in the past and I cannot change it or go back so I have to try and stop reliving it. It is easier said than done. I had to stop playing the same script in my mind repeatedly. I had to ask myself, 'did I reflect on what I could have done better?" Was it in my control? What do I plan to do differently TODAY to better prepare for my TOMORROW?*

*If I sat around TODAY, reliving my YESTERDAY while drowning in my guilt, shame, and mistakes, I am missing such an amazing opportunity TODAY to set myself up for my TOMORROW.*

*It is ok if I could not pull through today, but I had to promise myself that I would not get stuck here. Mom always told me; "you get a few hours to lay in that pity* bed but then get your ass up and figure out your next move." Before you move, find time to quiet your thoughts to hear from God or whoever/whatever you worship. SMILE, you are beautiful.

My loves, as I share my story with you, try not to sell yourself short, be who you are called to be so your TOMORROW self will thank your TODAY self for not being stuck in your mess with your YESTERDAY self. DO YOU UNDERSTAND what I am saying???

#selfdetermination #helpmefixourcrowns #neverforgetwhothef👑ckyouare

❤️Queesh

# Everyday Introduces New Opportunities...

*Hellllooooo today!! Believe me, when I say this, every day introduces new opportunities to us when we allow our hearts to open and accept all the things that GOD HAS IN STORE FOR OUR LIFE. When we say, "yes" to a new day with gratitude in our hearts and accept this way of living, we have the success of expanding our universe and opening our minds. We open ourselves to the unbelievable, limitless thoughts, and opportunities for ourselves and others around us. So, say, "yes" to today with gratitude. Every day I am so thankful for another day and another opportunity to be used!*

*#embracenewchallenges #beyou
#begreat #sayyestoyourself*

❤️*Queesh*

# Foundation...

*B*efore you continue with this snippet my loves, do me a quick favor and search the internet for the meaning of foundation.

Now, once you find it and understand it, what does it mean to you? Do you understand what foundation mean as it relates to your life?

This is typically where I always start and is often my go-to place no matter what I am facing throughout my journey. This is me. This is you. This is us.

Our foundation is just that, it is simply our grounded place. It was created before we were born. It shaped us. It developed us. It was deposited into us as children even when we could not make our own decisions. As least, this is how it feels in my journey. As we get older, we continue to build on our foundation, but we can never go back and change it. It is our foundation where it all began. It is a space we can frequent when we are trying to put things *into perspective. I embraced not being afraid to go back to obtain answers for myself when I felt lost. I had to trust it, dig deeper, breathe, learn to understand it, and apply it to areas where I needed it the most.*

*This is the inner and outer you. Everything that you have gained in life started here. You can evolve and elevate BUT this place will ALWAYS be your starting ground. This is what I kept hearing. This is a big part of your why. Why you decided to change. Why you go as hard as you do. Why you continue to remain focused. Why your 'not now' is just as good as a 'yes.' Why it hurt today but you are still fighting tomorrow. Why you are optimistic. Why you believe in a higher calling. Why you understand it is not about you. It is why you strive!!! Good, bad, or indifferent, this is your foundation. I love it!*

*Instead of trying to change it or regretting it my loves, I had to think about what brought me here so often. I found myself thinking through what I gained every time I came back to this place. When I found myself disliking this place or space, I had to be honest with myself and ask, "why?" Once I answered myself, I needed to deal with my skeletons to move to my happy place. It was not as bad once I faced it. Thank you, Lord!*

*Without a foundation, how do we begin to build? Unfortunately, the way life is designed we did not have much say in our foundation, but we can help others and generations after us as we navigate through our journeys to bring change. How would we know where to start or what to stand on to build our legacy to fulfill our purpose without our foundation? Even when I did not have all the answers, I began or should I say, I learned how to embrace and continue to build on what I had. It brings me joy that we get to paint the pages of our story and live our truth. No journey on earth is a fairy tale but in God's eyes it is perfect. That filled my heart.*

*I love you!! I love us!! Keep growing and glowing*

♥Queesh

# Is Life Unfair...

*H*ey babes... I hear people often say that life is or can be unfair... what do you think about that? How do you feel about that? I thought that a few times throughout this journey of mine as well... I mean if I can be honest, I have said, "God, that's so unfair" ... going through bs or snippets of no... I thought geeezzzz how f'ing unfair... the more you live (like our elders would say) the more you think differently by the cards you are dealt... It also depends on how you view the things that you're going through... what kind of cards were you dealt and how did or do you play them... life can seem unfair depending on how it's viewed or perceived through the lens of our own eyes... how did you get to the point of feeling so down? Feeling like it is truly unfair? Was it something that you gave away or was something taken away from you? When I ask that question, I am referring to your internal power, your purpose, or your drive? Did you stop and ask yourself where do you go from here? Going nowhere or *giving up is not even an option so if we can, STOP right there and figure out our next step or steps... while you are thinking through this, please understand that baby steps are ok and continue moving. If we can just use the unfairness that we have defined in our mind for energy and take advantage and thrive.*

*Go ahead and write it down, create a plan, stay focused, and excel.*

*Life may seem unfair today but think about what our future holds... reflect here in 6-12 months and let me know if you still feel the same way.*

*Go and be great... throughout our journey, favor will not always be fair, but our destiny is our destiny... I love you so much... go and leave your footprints and do not get caught up in what does not matter.*

*#JustQueesh*

# Daily Regulation...

HELLOOOOOO!!!!!! I am so elated to share this topic; I believe that sometimes I have not always understood what it truly means to regulate. I met this guy through my organization that specialized in applying neuroscience to improve and sustain business and individual results. He was hired as a consultant by the company I work for. He committed himself to our success over the next few years working close with us. When I met him, he shared with me and others, how he would fast while traveling on business throughout the day and would only eat once a day. He decided that one meal would be dinner. I thought to myself, hmmm, ok, if that works for him then so be it, who am I to judge? Friends, listen, I am eating and not skipping one meal. I like my calories! Throughout the day he would only drink coffee and water. I never saw him eat a darn thing, but let me tell you, this guy had such a positive yet different (I am not judging just saying) vibe *that intrigued me to want to know more about his daily rhythm. I felt like, I needed some of whatever he had and mix a little in my flow. I never asked at first, but I sure was observing him with a keen eye. As we continued through our contract with this company, of course, our relationship began to develop, and he shared some of his stories. His likes, his dislikes, what was fun, different challenges, experiences, etc. etc.*

*So, the more he shared with us from different articles, countless examples, team-building exercises, etc. it all began to connect. Now, I was able to see a clearer picture. I begin to understand some of the tactics he used to keep himself aligned with his goals and things that needed to be carried out for him to fulfill or regulate himself.*

*Many of us, have daily routines that we do every day, and we never understand why they are so important for our wellbeing until we miss one or change up our plan. These things are needed to keep us aligned, balanced, and focused on the TASK at hand.*

*Although this insert is not as deep as the others, I wanted to share it with you all. I have rededicated myself to ensuring that I have a weekly routine that encompasses my devotion time and that I continue to do things that bring ME joy.*

*I have my coffee or tea daily and I try to never skip a beat. If you drink coffee or tea, can you imagine it is noon and suddenly you realize something is missing? You knew something was wrong but could not put your finger on it. Do any of you take walks? Do you sit on your back deck? Sit on your front porch? Sit and read in the bathroom? Catch up on social media? Listen to the news? Stare at what you plan to wear in your closet. Do you have prayer time? Daily special calls? No matter what it is, it is a part of your daily rhythm, and it is needed for you to regulate yourself to be the BEST version of you that you can be. So, do not forget the small yet important responsibility that we owe to ourselves. If you do not do it, no one else will. When we do not do this or miss what feeds our soul, we begin to disconnect and become discombobulated.*

*When you find yourself lost or confused or simply off, think about what is missing from your daily regimen and then incorporate that activity. Drop everything you are doing and make it happen to get yourself back on track! I see YOU over there regulating and ish! It looks good on you! Do more of this for you.*

*Finish strong my loves, finish strong. We will never be able to repeat this day, we only get one chance.*

*Love Queesh*❤️

# *Why...*

*hy do we often find ourselves running from our
problems only to return to face them all over
again. Many times, we might not face it again until 5
years later when something triggers us or suddenly it
jumps out of the closet, like oh hey... hello... I am back...
or, oh hey, guess what... I never left... When we are on
the run from it, it is as if we are 'free' just for a moment
and it allows us to catch our breath to regain ourselves.
When I am going through things and do not deal with
them face to face, my first thought is to always just get
away... Shut it out... get busy... find something to do to
block it out... This has been my recipe for years... When
I am trying to deal with the problem head on it causes
anxiety, fear, and uncertainty of how things will turn
out... This is me battling with myself while leaving out
faith, hope, and God's word. I understand when we are
going through challenges, it can feel like a conundrum
of feelings racing thru our body's, sending us spiraling*

*down until we cannot catch ourselves, although we are trying so hard to gain our composure. For a second we can catch our breath and before we know it, we are going down yet again. I continue to ask myself, "why is that?" It is not the end of the world, and it is only one area in our life, but it affects so many other dynamics within our world. Until we cross that bridge or deal with it face on, it will arise again. When left unresolved, it just festers and continue to grow like mold. As I get to know myself better, I continue to pray day in and day out knowing that one day this will all be a memory. All a memory that will make me a wiser person in the future to share with others. All I can think of is what a blessing knowing that I survived the storm and now can share that with someone else to help pull them through. That is always my hope. For now, I will continue to stay here until I rise. I know that this picture is bigger than me. I had to go through some ish for me to have this realization in my life. I know I will have more mountains to climb but with God surrounding and holding me, I know now, THIS is part of my WHY!*

*Love Queesh*♥

# A Sincere Apology to my Mother...

As a young adult maturing into adulthood but so far away, there were many moments when I thought I had it all figured out and understood everything that was taking place. Friends, if I can be honest with you all this is how I remember feeling during the ages of 18-24ish. I recall thinking I had everything figured out including raising children. Can you recall a time when you did not understand certain decisions your parents made, and you questioned their judgment? If you did not, I did. There were many decisions my mother had to make at a young inexperienced age for me and my brother growing up, that I questioned. There were many decisions that my mother had to make as a wife in a blended family, that I admired. There were major decisions that my mother had to make after a divorce and the fact that she had to be a single parent again after being married for over 15 years with my younger siblings, that I questioned. There were even more decisions my mother had to make as *her children became older and decided to venture out in life that I questioned and admired. Like when to let go, when to be there, when to tell us the truth and when to just love from afar.*

*I questioned so many decisions that she had to make not realizing or understanding at that time she was doing the best that she could with what she had. Today, I can relate more to all the decisions she had to make, and I wholeheartedly understand and praise her for each one that she made. Mother, I know you never cared who understood your reasoning or what anyone said about it, but I want to publicly acknowledge that I get it and you made many decisions that some people will never have the courage to make. Your decisions helped mold us into who we are today. We are your amazing children all hand-selected for a woman that stands 4 ft 11 inches that is our idol. You are the epitome of strength and the glue that holds us together. You taught us to love, how to build a relationship with God, how to love others, how to hustle, never settle, always find a way, never make excuses for our actions, own up to our shit, learn from our mistakes, do better, take care of our families, learn to forgive, and help others when we're appointed. As we grow older, we understand all our roles and responsibilities.*

*Until you go through what your parents grew through try not to judge them for the decisions, they had to make without sitting down and talking with them to understand their side.*

*QUEESH*❤️

**Anquesha Tillman**

Never Forget Who The F*ck You Are

# *Awareness...*

# Crystal Davis...

Hello, my friends. Have you ever had a special person in your life, that maybe no one in your family knew about? You do not hang with this person, but you may mention them periodically in conversations. You also share a pure genuine relationship that is unbiased. This person is dear and near to your heart for being authentic. You can be who you are with this person, no holding back, no judging, pure openness with each other. That is who Crystal Davis was or will always be to me. As her manager, I was always able to be authentic. I am not saying you cannot be yourself; you have to be able to separate your business role from your personal affairs and be selective on the things that you share during your conversations.

As her friend, Crystal allowed me to be me. She welcomed me, she encouraged me, she inspired me, and she always came in my office at the right time for me to take my mind away from work when a much-needed break was called for. I knew Crystal for over 10 years, and she loved the Lord. She never wavered who she was or who she served throughout her life. She remained focused on what God called her to do and was very obedient. Crystal was determined to beat her illness; she never gave up even when the odds were stacked against her. She continued to fight and believe in a higher calling throughout her lifelong journey. Her faith never wavered; this is what I admired in her. She took her no in life and looked at them as 'not now.' Understanding that God is a God of no mistakes and whatever is done it is his will.

Crystal was always willing to lead her peers in a very stern but very polite manner. I recall asking her several times to be a leader on the floor amongst her peers and she would always say, "I got you." I never knew what she did or if she did anything until the day of her home going. Her peers said so many remarkable things about her detailing how she kept them focused and in line. Her voice was exceptionally soft, but firm and she was/is well respected.

She passed a week after her birthday in 2019. We briefly spoke about her making sure that she celebrate with her twin sister and enjoy her birthday, I recall telling her, "Don't go home and go to sleep... go and hang out, you owe yourself this." I remember her saying, they were past due spending time together. I never got a chance *to hear about her night with her sister until her mother shared the details with me after her passing.*

She was my girl… when I wrote this pearl it has been a year and there is not a week that goes by that I do not think about her or any of our conversations. Some of the things that I go through I am constantly wishing we could chat and laugh and tell each other to listen to Rick Ross and let our inner thug out.

*Until we meet again my friend, you are forever missed. I love you!*

*#MyCrystal #GodFearing #SoftSpoken #YouEarnedUrWings*

# I Love Us...

So, at first, I thought about only sharing this message with a few selected people via text message but decided to write a pearl in this journal. One day I received a message, and I could not sleep so I ended up finding a book to start reading. That morning during online service all the messages connected (of course). In the messages, they all focused around the struggle between the person that we are and the person that we are becoming. Thank you, Pastor Touré Roberts. Listen, who we are today is still a part of who we have been all our life. Certain points throughout our journey we eventually recognize that we are evolving. What a great feeling. We make many efforts to focus on who we want to be in the bigger scheme of life as we mature. As I was transitioning through this season, I noticed I was beginning to become more intentional and there was a constant battle internally that will always be based on my outside factors. There is no right or *wrong way to get to our next chapter but continue to be intentional as we evolve.*

*I was only going to share this message with my family because there is never any judgment from them, I think lol, it is MY safe place, and they are my biggest fans. Many of us may share that commonality. As I was thinking about sharing this topic, that small but loud voice politely reminded me that I was/am strategically placed I felt that where I am today. I have so many people that pour into me personally and they share tough and challenging life experiences with me. Sometimes they look to me to solve their problem and throughout my journey being transparent and honest it is taking me further and deeper in many relationships. Many times, in the moment I do not have much to say or offer except for a listening ear. In the beginning I did not know that was ok because I felt as though I always had to respond. As I go through this journey my overall desire is not to judge or mix my emotions with their truth. I have done this plenty times before where their truth became my personal problem. I know that was selfish of me and I am not afraid to share my truth. Someone special told me, "Don't take my journey personal, this is mine and I'm just sharing with you." I was also told, "me being open and honest with you does not benefit this relationship and I'll never open up to you again." Hmmmmm, I thought at first, but ok then.*

*I am learning the roles to play and how to put myself in their shoes and really dive into what their experiencing and how it felt for them. That was truly my aha moment combined with things I am continuing to learn from the bible. This made me realize two especially important things; 1. I was still growing, and I was far from where I thought I was silly me and 2. confessing one's wrong starts with being ok knowing you are wrong and being delivered by God first because we are all at different points in our life. The statement never left my mind and made me think and begin asking myself questions that allowed me to reflect. I had to ask myself, why was I so upset, angry, and bothered by this? After much prayer, reading, and putting God's word into action that part I started evolving again. I really started learning to pull myself and my emotions out of other people issues this was tough. Even though it hurt me, removing myself out of the picture allowed me to see things deeper. That deeper view will take you places and reveal God's power. Now as I listen to individuals confiding in me, if the word is not delivered in that moment, I take the time to say, "this is heavy and I'm going to need time to pray and meditate and find the word that God delivers to me for you during this time, but in the meantime I'm here for you to listen but continue your journey and don't give up." "Don't forget to be nice to yourself for nothing is perfect and everything is always and only perfected in God's timing."*

*Loves, this one insert in the book was not planned but heavy on my heart this morning. We battle things internally and do not really know what to do with all of it rising at us at once. As we transform into who we are called to be, understand that you are only battling with yourself. Give yourself love and courage to continue to build on the Today you for a better Tomorrow you. Nothing is perfected overnight.*

*Queesh loves you*

# Don't Put Yourself in a Box...

If you do not mind, may I please grab your attention for a second? I had to learn not to place myself in a box and I am asking you not to do that as well. Everyone else is already doing that to us. Well, not everyone but during my journey I have experienced and created stories in my mind where people will judge you subconsciously, so you are already there when it comes to them and yourself. So, if we can, steer away from doing that to ourselves. Why add to what everyone else may already be thinking? If we do that as well to ourselves, what will set us apart from the rest? How will we overcome this false status of ourselves that could be slowly defining who we are in an unrealistic view that belittles who we really are? I had to realize that when I was putting myself in a box, I was robbing myself of my future and the true person I was called to be. I was limiting myself when I should have been reaching for the stars. I could never reach for the stars in a closed box, right? I had to be ok with who I *was at that moment and understand and embrace who I was becoming. I had to learn to be unapologetic. How to be brave. How to be courageous. How to be me. How to be kind. That is the best gift that I could give myself. When I learned to transform this way of thinking, I began giving the universe the best version of me. When I started believing in myself in a higher light, I somehow knew others would as well. There is always someone watching you. Get out of that box, leave a legacy, and change a life or two! What else is there to offer?*

*I love you! Now get out of that box and go be great at being the best version of you there is.*

*#DontLimitYourself #BeGreat #GetOutOfThatBox*

❤️*Queesh*

# Try Not to be Confused...

At some point I begin to have an optimistic view that was full of hope that this world would be full of people that will not judge each other for all the things we choose to do randomly or go through throughout our lives.... I found myself saying yes today and no tomorrow... I wanted to leave today but stay tomorrow... I found that you may believe today and not tomorrow... you may be super excited today but down tomorrow... I had to learn that it was ok to be who I was in that moment. I had to learn how to remove the confusion and stop being so hard on myself for not making the same decision day after day. Loves, it is ok to be you and do as you please. You are the pilot of your plane. Try to always remember, you are transforming and evolving so do not beat yourself up or toggle within yourself to make you feel as if you are invaluable, not worth it, or a mess. Even if you are a mess at that moment, embrace your mess, own your *mess, crown your mess, acknowledge your mess, and keep trying to elevate yourself. While going through these various emotions this is between you and God to figure out and you will. I had to stop focusing on others or what they thought or how they felt. I just hoped they would be forgiving and not judgmental but had to always remember they did not have a hell or heaven to place me in. I knew there would be moments when I could not get it right and I should not be depending on myself because I am not in charge. We I always find a way to jack things up. I am laughing at many things I recall jacking up. I notice when I take my hands off or stop thinking I am in control and depend on Jesus, it always lands me in the right place at the right time.*

*My loves, as we chat and reflect on this chapter, think about what confused you about yourself recently. Take yourself out of that perfect box that you have created. Stay here for a moment. During this time, quiet the noise and be honest with yourself, show yourself grace and be cool with who you are in this space. The more you accept yourself you will notice that you will have more joy, happiness, and laughter about things you are going through and decisions you make. Laugh about it and smile about it, this is your journey. Live it how you want but be* kind and remember this is not about you or me, there is a higher calling for your life. Smile, laugh, pray, and sip but please do not judge.

Love Queesh 💗

# Sister, Pastor, Sarah Jakes Roberts...

It was the summer of 2018 when I unofficially introduced my team to Pastor Sarah Jakes Roberts's "Mind Your Business Ministries". While everything about this was wrong, "typically" in corporate America, it was perfect timing for me and my team. I recall getting ready to beef up my staff for our summer volume and my team was doing the most. If you do not understand what doing the most is, in this situation they were being very immature in my eyes and did not take accountability for their actions. Day after day I was receiving complaints about this coworker, this manager did not do this, this manager did not say good morning, she looked at me crazy, why do the other departments get to wear spandex and Ugg's and we cannot, why do the other centers blah blah blah blah. I had enough!

Let me start by painting the picture for you friends, I started my daily routine which starts each morning at 5 am Monday through Friday to get to work no later than 8 am. I lived fifty-two miles away from my job and I sit in traffic anywhere from 1 to 2 hours on any given day and that is only one way. This can be incredibly stressful on a person that also has demands to meet at work and after work with a family of five.

I started listening to Sarah early in 2018 and immediately fell in love with her work and her voice. I love how she was obedient and how God was using her to bring light that glorified him. While I begin listening to her, I remember thinking, "wow, I could relate to her." Instantly, we became sisters and best friends. Listening to her I would hear other ladies refer to her as sister and as a friend as well and I just thought to myself, "I'm not sure how this is going to work once they understand how connected we are, but I'm ok with sharing and embracing this sisterhood." I became a supporter and began sharing her platform.

Finally, on this day, I arrived at work, parked my car, and glanced at my emails, as I did each morning to make sure nothing caught me by surprise when I walked into the office. As I was scrolling through my emails, there was that one email that just took me over the top. I walked into the building, dropped my bags in my office, powered up my laptop, and scheduled an impromptu meeting off the floor, next to HR. I had no clue which direction this meeting was going to take, but we needed a "come to Jesus' meeting," quickly. I mistakenly added people to the meeting that were not on my direct team BUT because of the mood I was in everyone was going to hear this message today. "Please come in, have a seat, and all eyes on me." I paced and pranced across the floor, sashaying from left to right with words spewing from my heart for them to hear. I meant every word I said on that day unapologetically with no regrets.

By the end of the meeting my team understood that we were in a Season of Eyes Forward and Mind Your Business. Too many times we are quick to tell each other what someone else was not or is not doing to our liking but dare not admit what they are lacking. Too many times we only look out for ourselves and could care less about others because seeing them fail was great. Too many times we forget that there is no I in team. I also shared a clip from Drumline, if we cannot be one band one sound, I do not want your negativity on my team. If you are not here to help this company win, let me know if you need to use me as a reference for your next job. I will do that for you. I will help you pack up your desk so that you can *be on a journey that makes you happy. You will not stay here and make the rest of the team miserable. Those of you that think you are hiding in the weeds; I will sniff you out because that is the season I am in and manage you out. When you come to this company each day, your role is to slide your badge, do your work with high ethics and integrity, help people, be kind, collect your coins and go home. Anything else is not required.*

*After this very intense meeting, I reported myself to HR and my manager just in case someone did not like what I said. It was a tough but needed conversation. I am still employed, and my team is still on a beautiful glowing and growing path. I have so many testimonies from individuals that left the company, and they are thriving to the fullest and making me so proud.*

*Many mornings Sarah kept me level-headed and many days commuting to work I enjoyed listening to her and the delegation. From what I hear in her podcast and as I watch her on YouTube her story is beautiful, and she is highly creative with the way she uses her experiences to share with people. The experiences she share are very relatable, but she also has the favor to connect with people and share God's teachings in an easy way. She could have easily just remained T.D. Jake's daughter, but she sought out to find her journey to fulfill her purpose. Based on her story she did not fall victim to her circumstances, and she continued to follow the path that was destined for her. Her walk is her walk, and she is vulnerable and brave enough to share with the world and not be ashamed. That is what we are called to do to help others see that it is ok and all a part of God's blueprint for us.*

*Many blessings to you and your family Sarah, thank you for your obedience.*

*♥Queesh*

# Don't be too Busy...

*A*re you that busy running errands, meeting unfulfilled deadlines, running to dead-end networking events, and filling in space that led you to places that do not matter when you look at the big picture in your life? Are you doing something that will bring you gratification eventually or is this business of yours just filling invaluable time that will catch up with you one day and leave you regretting the time that you wasted? Do you think that being that busy all the time is healthy? If you are too busy working so hard all your life, when do you have time to enjoy what matters? The older I get, the more I realize that time does not sit still for anyone. My friends, I had to ask myself all these questions because there will be a time and place for everything. I began to dig deeper to understand my boundaries and the importance of balance by not being too busy with invaluable things and people.

At the age of twenty-four, I resigned from a stable job of 7 years, ended a 7-year relationship, broke my *apartment lease, moved in with my mom & my siblings in a 1200 square foot home and shared a room that could barely fit twin bunk beds and a dresser for me and my boys for 6 months. During that time, I was mentally preparing to move to another state that was 6 hours away. I would be away from everything and everyone I loved. Two months after moving, I was still searching for employment and a place to live. My savings ran out and my credit dropped from 700+ to under 500. During this time, I was getting very discouraged and angry. I started digging in the past and began turning over rocks to find things I never healed from. I was disappointed and angry at both of my fathers; my car broke down and then repossessed. My children were still in my home state between my grandmother's house and with their father. I was living with my bestie and sharing a room with my 5-year-old nephew and 2-year-old niece. During my journey, I realized I could not fail, I set out to accomplish so much but at this moment I had NO idea what was next. This journey forced me to BELIEVE in a higher calling, it taught me not to depend on myself because she, that would be me, had nothing for us but determination and faith that was all God needed to move. I KNOW now that this was my destiny based on the relationship that I am continuing to build with our father. There was no grandmother, no mother, no aunts, or cousins around the corner to help. This journey was about learning and understanding who and what I must accomplish to understand my purpose, which would not come until years later. All I knew was that I just could not fail, do you understand what I am saying? I had to keep pushing, I had to keep going, I HAD to find my way. I knew God did not lead me here to this place where I was standing for nothing. During my transition of trying to find a job to obtain some income because I had nothing, I was offered three jobs that I was willing to take to help me stabilize, get some cash in my pocket, and get on my feet. I started working at some job in a warehouse and the cubicles were no more than four feet wide. I was making cold calls that I do not even remember what it was about, and I did not make it past day 1. I was offered a job thru another company but before I could accept the position, my old manager in Tampa called me to ask me if I would like to work for my prior organization again in one of the branch offices. I said, "absolutely, yes, yes, yes." He said, "the job is yours, call this number and you are good to go." #Favor*

*4 months later, I had a place to live, and my children were with me in our new home. We had no furniture aside from their beds that I saved from my old apartment. For the next year, I slept on an air mattress that my grandmother bought for me. My TV was prompted up on a storage container and we were ready for the ride. Throughout my journey, I enrolled in school and begin working on my degree while employed.*

*Two years later I was laid off and started working for another company within two weeks. Favor is not fair, was all I could think of. Taking this job, my pay increased by $3.00 an hour and we had unlimited overtime. I continued school and completed my bachelor's degree in 2009.*

*During this time, I took care of my kids and worked two jobs. I sacrificed a lot to get to where we needed to be with God surrounding me. One full-time job and one part-time job just to be able to pay the bills. I did this for about 4 years. Once I finished my degree, I was reminded that I did not sacrifice all that I did to be stagnant. So, what is next? I had to kick it into gear. Always looking to step out on faith, here we go and over the next 10 years, I was promoted repeatedly.*

*When I speak about my promotions, many of you may think about titles and salary increases. I did too as I was going through it but when I look back and reflect on my promotions, everything was to bring glory to God. God took me to a place that gave me access to a diverse group of individuals on various levels, social classes, gender, called me to help break chains all while teaching me to be kind and love his people.*

*Back in 2006, I remember sitting on my bed and I remember being so broke that I just cried and prayed aloud to my God to bless me in a way that I never have to depend on anyone financially and that he would carry me and my kids and supply our wants and needs. Every time I think about this moment, my eyes fill up with tears. During that time, it was me hurting, when I cry now, I am thinking about God's grace and mercy. During that time in my life, I was scraping pennies. I could never work two weeks in a row because I did not have enough gas money after Wednesday to get to work on that Thursday before payday Friday. There were so many times I had to just call off. Eventually, as I was going through emotional turmoil, I ended up taking a leave from work repeatedly to gain my self-composure and get myself together. That was the only thing I knew to do at that moment. I had to ensure I did not have a breakdown trying to get everything done and take care of my boys.*

*Friends, 15 years later, I found myself hungry for more... wanting to help on more of a spiritual connection and having a burning fire on the inside of me waiting to explode like a volcano. I had to realize that the chapter I was in or book I was writing was about over. God has something bigger for me and I can feel it. If I can share anything from all of this, pay attention to the signs and things that are taking place in your life and LISTEN. Learn to BE STILL! Do not be too anxious about things that seem wrong and do not always think you can fix them right away. Try to ask God to reveal your test to you. Give things time and your undivided attention. Quiet your mind, find your balance, trust your gut, move slow (but move) and conquer it all. There is something that we all must share as a part of our journey and calling to help someone. Do not miss your opportunity being too busy on the things that do not matter.*

*#ILOVEYOU #STOPBEINGSOBUSYDOINGTHINGSTHATDONTMATTER #KNOWYOURCALLING #BLESSWHOYOUCAN #KNOWTHESIGNS #QUIETYOURMIND*

*Queesh loves you*❤

Never Forget Who The F*ck You Are

# Be Careful not to Succumb to the Noise...

The trivial things around us that may seem to take over our thoughts and seem important is what I like to call Noise. When you learn to silence the noise, you can hear loud and clear. Anything that may cause you to lose sleep or cause unwarranted stress, but you know it is out of your control is a distraction to get you off your path is what I call, Noise. I tell myself, stay the course and remain focused. There may be things going on in your life that you cannot seem to shake, decide on, or figure out. During my journey, I have learned to start each morning giving thanks to God and allow him to guide my thoughts on things that he want/need from me on that day. If I focus on that, I have learned that my clarity will come. Try not to fall victim to the noise. Remember to give it time and trust the process.

♥Queesh

# I Didn't Follow my Own Rules...

So, yeah, that happened... Have you ever done something and then look at yourself in the mirror and simply say, "Hey you, you knew better?" How many times have we worked on perfecting THIS, you ask yourself? You even tell yourself, "This opportunity will NEVER happen again any time soon. In that moment, it feels as if the opportunity would never present itself again.

Even though I may have failed the test, didn't take my own advice, and knew better but didn't do better; this was a growth moment for me. By acknowledging I failed the test was a testament to my growth. Friends, we are still growing and learning and that is the point that matters the most. We all have these moments so do not beat yourself up for failing (in your eyes). Look for the positive in every situation and tell yourself you are progressing.

Ugggggghhhhh but still we think to ourselves... Our actions and decisions always lead to our very own *consequences and what is to come. They can be good or bad and here we stand. Learning from them. Reflecting on the past. Practicing more to regulate ourselves and control our emotions to avoid the same mistake from happening again. If you do not get it right the next time, be easy on yourself. We will learn from them eventually, right? I mean eventually, that is our hope.*

*Follow your inner voice...take your advice... We know better and we will do better...*

*Queesh*

# Make Sure You Value Your "No"...

Friends, I believe this would be a great topic of discussion over a nice cup of coffee, tea, or your favorite beverage. This passage is not built on collecting data or surveying people, it is only constructed around my truth and my experiences. If you do not agree with them as you are reading this information, remember this is the beauty of everyone being unique.

When you are told 'no' how does that make you feel? Do you want to give up? Do you feel rejected? Does it drive you to try harder? Do you seek feedback? Do you appreciate your no? Think about it, how exactly do you handle your no?

When you are told, yes, how does it make you feel? Overjoyed? Ecstatic? On top of the world? Do you want to push even harder for the next level? Do you seek feedback? Do you appreciate your yes? Think about it, how exactly do you handle your yes's.

Why would your no be just as important as your yes? Really spend some time here to think about both answers and opportunities. How do they both shape you? Do you think they both shape you? If so, why or why not?

Stay here for a moment and let's check in later.

Love Queesh❤️

# Painful, Powerful Growth Moments...

# Gracefully Broken...

Hello, my loves, there will be things in life that make you feel like you have invested all your sweat, blood, and love into. When things do not align with what YOU thought it was or how YOU thought it should be did you feel as if your world had ended. I had many moments that broke me down to a point that humbled me even more as I tried to figure them out. How did I get here and why did this happen to me, was a constant ask to myself. We have all had that one, two, three, or however many disappointments in life. I call them disappointments because at that moment that is exactly how I felt as I was going through them. It did not feel like something I should have been experiencing based on how I uphold myself in whatever situation I am faced with. I had to dive into those feelings and think about how I felt at that moment. I felt like I was bamboozled into some foolishness and I tried to figure out how did I get there. We may even ask ourselves, days later, "what should I do." I recall many *times, saying, 'Lord speak to me."  The hurt was deeper than I could have ever imagined in my life. My loves, this was just the beginning of another transformation. Man, Gracefully Broken. I remember listening to Tasha Cobb singing Gracefully Broken, I played the song repeatedly in my car, I added this song to my playlist, and it continued to help change my perspective on how I viewed things and how I continued to deal with life. I never turned away, I never wanted to run away but I wanted to ask why? How? Is this real or is it a dream? Eventually, I learned to praise and give thanks while going through each of my challenges. That does not mean everything was easy or that the tears stop flowing. Life just started looking different from the new set of lenses I was wearing. I had to redirect my focus on what mattered the most in my life. That was me seeking God, listening for his voice and being obedient. Everything else was just noise and a distraction that inevitably turned into a win for me. As with everything else, I learned, there is a process and a cycle that we will continue to go through in every situation we are faced with. If we can remember this while going through it, I believe that we will be able to handle things a little easier. We cannot stay down forever; we came into this situation, and we must trust that we will come out a different person. A stronger, wiser person. Take the time and do not be afraid to deal with the emotions as they transpire to help you heal and grow.*

*Be excited about this transition even though you do not know the end. If you trust in God fully, you know that he (you) will win. Gracefully Broken, thank you. Keep Growing and Glowing my loves. The best is yet to come.*

*#LoveQueesh*❤️

# Was I Not Enough...

Was I not enough? Did you see me? Did you love me? Did you remember who I was? Hell, did I remember who I was? Do I know who I am? Was I lost? Were you lost? Was I too young to understand? Did you forget about me? Did you remember me? Was I not enough? Did I do something wrong? Did I fail you? Did I not meet your expectations? I promise I tried even when I did not know what I was doing, I promise I tried. I wish I could have been more... I wished I would have cried a little harder... a little louder... if so, things would have been different... Hello, it is me again. Did you see me? Did you feel me? Did you need me as much as I needed you? I cried for you... I begged you to stay... I think. Maybe I cried quietly... I was forced to be strong... I was forced to do it on my own... the pressure was real... I had to create my path... I had to survive... I tried... I failed... I succeeded... HEY!!! I was created for you... I was made by you... you created me, then you deserted me... I was angry... I was *mad... I was hurt... I was confused.... you left me to be alone... you left me to face this world on my own... I could not reach you... Here you stand again... I am scared... HEY! You did not see me... you did not need me as I needed you... did you hear me when I said I cried for you... Damn it!! I cried for you... DAMN, I wanted to be with you... I cried beside you... I cried in your arms... HEY! Did you love me? Ohhhhhh yes, yes, yes... I know you loved me... I know you cared... I now understand that you were busy fighting your own battles... it had nothing to do with me, personally... your love runs deep for me then and your love runs deep for me now...  it is ok, I forgave you... I forgave myself... I gave myself Grace... I forgive you... you were running your race... you had to sort through some stuff... God had to get your attention... life is crazy, right!?! Now we sit and laugh... now we sit and pray... now we sit and talk... we kept pushing through to see another day... we kept fighting... We did not give up... it makes more sense now...each day gets better... Our faith is stronger... we support each other... Our relationship is growing... Hey, continue to let your light shine... Do not be afraid... I am watching you... I am proud of you... you are our hero... I love you... I love me... I love our stories... I thank God for you... Thank you, Jesus! Thank you, God!*

*#myjourney #mystory #mytears #mymemories
#mygrowth #growingupwithoutdad
#sisterlove #fallinginlove #beingvulnerable
#facingmytruth #overcomingfear*

♥*Queesh*

# The Closet...

The closet... the closet... the closet... When I first started this chapter, I was going through a very dark moment in my life. All-day long as a mother, a partner, a daughter, a friend, a manager, etc. I had to wear this cape that portrayed me as if I was superwoman. By no means did I want this title or persona but, as we all do in life, we do what we must do to survive. At the end of each day when all my motherly blessings and duties were complete, I found myself in the closet. I found myself praying on my knees or lying flat on my stomach. Many times, no words were coming out of my mouth, just tears flowing down my face, hurt all throughout my body and a face full of slob and snot. The only thing that I could do with the strength I had left was to cry and call on the name of Jesus. I remember so vividly how the tears flowed down my face like a river. I remember how bad the pain hurt, it felt as if I was being cut with a knife and left to die. When I think back, this was not my first experience *being in the closet. During that time, I joined a prayer line with my grandmother. Lord, I was not ready for what you had in store for me. The experience of feeling the power of God move was amazing. It was an experience I never witnessed before. Not only did I admire their love for God, but their prayers moved through my soul.*

*I use this space to escape, to meditate, and to get a piece of quietness. The more my relationship developed with God, the more I read and focused on his word. The more I read, the more I understood. The more I focused on feeding my inner man the more I understood there was a higher calling and a better reward. Even during affliction, I had the realization that I could not give up no matter how much it hurt. The significance of the closet changed my life forever.*

*If you do not have a closet to use for your space, you can create a unique place where you can rededicate yourself to your purpose. It is well worth it. Going through the changes does not always feel good but please be sure to reflect, be optimistic, and celebrate your gains. Have hope, my friends.*

*#findyouacloset #quietthenoise #meditate*

❤️*Queesh*

# *Feeling Numb...*

*H*ave you ever felt numb? I remember when I was flat out numb, stupid numb, numb-numb... I did not know if I was coming or going. Have you ever been there before? I mean like blanked out of everything type numb. While I was experiencing this feeling, I still knew everything that was going on around me, but I still could not feel anything. It was as if I was in a total state of shock or disbelief. I recall even making bad decisions or decisions that did not define or align with who I was. The emotions came in waves. I was hurt but not angry. I was just flat out, HURT. It took a while for my feelings, thoughts, heart, mind, soul, and body to all catch up with each other. It was like I was stuck in a daze. Stuck in space. Stuck in the zone. Stupid stuck. I was not comprehending what took place around me, but I was still able to navigate daily. I hope that makes sense. I kept trying to make sense of the situation but found that I was asking myself each morning; "is this real?" "Did this just happen?" and "how *did I get here?" I kept replaying the same situation over and over only to relive the prior day.*

*This season or test lasted for a long time. I believe that all my test come from my God. I believe that you will have to take the same test over and over and over until you pass. You cannot move on to the next level or chapter until you pass where you stand. Each level God entrusts us with so much more.*

*Over the next however many months of reading the word and creating devotion time, my outlook and understanding of the word began to shift. Throughout this process, I started to understand this was already scribed in my blueprint. I was being gracefully broken and it allowed me to be in that space, at that time for a higher more impactful calling down the road. I was strategically placed. Lord, I thank you!*

*As I was going through this test in my life, which was life changing, I begin to come to grasp with reality. Slowly but surely, I begin to snap out of it and things slowly began to fall into place. What I experienced was way over my head because there were so many more tests and seasons that I would be approaching, and I had no clue about what was to come. While taking a deeper dive into the word, reflecting on my journey, and acknowledging my emotions there was a comforting peace that overcame me. I was able to think with more rationale and the funny thing is that my focus shifted away from that small yet impactful bump in the road in my journey. If I had to do it all over again, I would invite that same test back into my life because it got me where I am today. At the time I had no clue how this would change my life for the better, but over the next few years, God revealed so much to me. I had to understand that this journey would not end in just a day. I had to understand that this was not about me. I had to understand that I was going through many different seasons and life lessons to prepare me for what was next. I had to learn to quiet the noise. I had to lose myself to find myself and humble myself.*

*I recall having a conversation with my mom daily for a month straight... just crying, I mean sobbing and explaining how much I was hurting... the pain was unbearable... I explained to her how I had to hold in my tears and be 'super mom'... how I had to fight the pain and be a 'super manager'... how I had to be 'superwoman' for everyone... how I could not recognize who I was... and so forth. My mom said to me one day in such a soft voice, "baby, it's time for you to get yourself together." I feel as if God delivered that word to her because she said this before but the way I heard it, it was different. That was the last night I cried like a child that did not know any better. I want you to imagine a child crying hysterically because you told them 'No,' they cannot have that fifth doughnut. Crying like it was the end of the world only to find out, it is not! Well, friends that was me. I had the ugly cry! The girl, what is wrong cry. I had the, I want to slap and tell you cut that mess out, cry! The, oh hunni, that is too damn much cry. After my mom dropped that in my spirit, my spirit man immediately said, "Say less, where's my Bible, it's time for me to deliver me from myself, I have some work to do."*

*Losing myself during this transition was the best thing that could have happened to me during this period in my life. I had to hit the wall just to realize this was bigger than me. It was by God's saving Grace, his word, his obedient servants, and my hunger for more of him that pulled me out. It was not a great feeling while I was going through it but, I am here to tell you friends, hang on and have hope and patience even during affliction. Whatever your hope is, keep it at the forefront of your mind and keep pressing forward. Do not lose sight of hope, use it as your promise and allow it to excite your future. This is your fuel. Stay focused and give thanks! Find someone to talk to, not just anyone, but a solid sounding board. Please do not keep it in. Keeping it in will only fester and harm you either now or later. Deal with it now if you can to be able to navigate in your later years. For me to understand now that God was equipping me for what was to come and all of that was never about me but more in line with how God would use me is priceless.*

❤️Queesh

# I'm Good, I'm Ok...

Friends, I know you are tired of reading about how much I cry, lol, but IDC!!! YOU are going to hear me out and receive the blessings that are covered in MY tears. My tears do not define me, so I allow them to flow whenever they want to no matter who is around watching. My tears help me heal and even when I might cry, please know, I'm ok. I may lay around and stare at the TV all day, but I am good. I may just get up and exercise until I cannot work out anymore, but I am good. When I am super stressed, my credit cards are pulled out and I buy everything I want, but I am ok. I may snap at the family including the fur babies and trust me I mean no harm when I do this, but I am good. I may not eat as I should, but I am ok.

I'm good and I'm ok does not mean that my pain is not there, it just means that in this life, this season, or moment I'm in, I have no choice but to be ok and to be good. There is a season for everything that you endure in life, and you must be ok going through things understanding that *your tomorrow is around the corner. Friends, we do not have time to sit still and watch the time go by. There is so much to be done according to your blueprint. When we are weak, we must find a greater strength from above that pushes and connects us greater and deeper to who he is. If you do not understand this or understand how to push through, please try to figure this out. You have 5 minutes each day to sit around and cry, but please learn how to produce even during this time. Every minute and hour count more than you know. So, while it may seem like on the outside looking in, oh she's a cry baby, oh she's weak, oh she's a mess. God is constantly using and pushing me to deliver on all things placed inside of me. Even when we are sleep, he is fighting our battles and clearing our paths.*

*So, when people ask you "how are you doing" and you know that you are having one of those days, it is ok to say, "I'm ok" or "I'm good" and say it with purpose.*

*Go out there and crush your goals! Smile, Laugh, Pray or Sip but Don't Judge!*

*Until next time, I love you!*

♥*Queesh*

# When I thought I Couldn't Hear...

This one hit different friends. This one started yet another powerful change in my life and a path that I know will bless me full circle. When I began writing this note to you all, I am not completely through this chapter of my life, but I wanted to share where I am currently standing. I am at the beginning, but I am sure I will have more to share later. For now, can we talk through this moment when I thought I could not hear the voice of God. You ever feel like you are stuck in a tunnel or better yet a dream. In this dream, you continue to play the same scene over and over in your head and you cannot seem to escape it. You pray about it, you meditate, you exercise, and you try to do everything in your power to avoid the thought. I felt as though I needed to get away and be alone so I could hear his distinct voice. I kept asking, "what are you saying to me, God?" "What are you telling me to do?" "Which way should I turn?" "Is this the right thing to do?" "Do I run away?" "Do I walk away?" "Do I lash out and act a damn fool?" Please say yes to this, just kidding "What is it that I'm supposed to do?"

I felt lost. I felt like I was stuck in twilight zone with no way out. This was not me; this is not what I do… uggghhhh why am I here?

I felt as though I could not feel God's presence. Was his voice already telling me exactly what to do or was my voice overpowering what I wanted to hear? My flesh and spirit were fighting internally. At that moment I was confused and when I feel as if I cannot hear God's voice clear and concise it is not good for me. I need to hear loud and clear to be able to move forward in everything I do. I just could not quiet my inner flesh and spirit man no matter how hard I tried. The message that I heard was overpowered by my two internal loved ones and I did not want to accept it during this time. It did not seem like it fit into the mysterious puzzle that I was putting 'back' together. That one puzzle piece or section throughout that chapter was weird.

I recall preparing for a trip away, as I pulled out of the driveway heading to my destination, I remember being so nervous taking a trip alone. I never traveled with sister girl forty-five, but she was with me on that trip. When I drove away from my house, I was shockingly at ease. It was not sister girl '45' that eased my mind it was God's presence.

When I arrived, I walked into my suite and my room had an astonishing wrap-around balcony (God knew I would spend a lot of time out there) and on this balcony, there were two chairs and a lounge chair. Perfect, right? RIGHT! After I settled in, I walked down to an onsite restaurant/bar, social distance style and grabbed dinner. Upon my arrival back in my room as I walked back out on the balcony, I witnessed a full rainbow; I have never seen one before and I am 39 years old. I was staying at a resort that was on a beach and the forecast was showing rain all weekend. Well, my loves, it only drizzled for about 20 minutes that weekend... smile.

$829.84 was the cost of this new experience for me. That was for 2 nights... that could have been a few pair of shoes if I just would have listened. Throughout this journey, learn to have patience hunni is what I kept telling myself.

Throughout my stay, I realized I was already hearing everything that I needed to hear while I was home. Even in my whirlwind I was reminded, you can hear me my child, do not ever think any problem is too big that I cannot handle. I AM! That is what God shared with me on the day... it was my confirmation that he is always with me *no matter what I am going through or where I am. That was priceless.*

*I will always be loud enough for YOU to recognize my voice, learn to silence the noise, trust your heart, lean on me, focus on what matters, and elevate.*

*You may have needed this break for yourself but know that I am omnipresent, regardless of what you think or how you feel... you are learning to decipher me during your storm... THIS PART! While you are learning this, you are also learning to silence the noise.*

*During this second in my life, I recall calling my grandmother and she did not answer. Now when I reflect on everything it was all planned out in advance to gratify the Lord. Jesus!*

*Keep leaning on me my child it is all destined to my design to bring glory to my kingdom. When you hit this moment in your life, your perspective on life shifts yet again.*

*#Queesh*❤️

# Shit Runs Deep...

*M*any moments will pass you by in life and you may never understand the moments until months, years, or even decades later... things that once was a blur is now meaningful to you and will also connect many dots for you in your "now" that may not have made sense "then."

During that time, you were naïve towards those feelings or thoughts. You may have thought about it for a second and it did not even bother you. You realized then that it did not make total sense. It is not until something triggers inside of you when that feeling crosses your path again. At that moment you realize that thing that took place in your past makes more sense to you now than it ever did before. For example, when I think about my daughter and her father's relationship, it is a relationship that I love to watch from the outside looking in because it was something that I missed (not was missing if that makes sense) as a little girl. I never knew what that feeling was like to be a daddy's girl. I never had that experience.

*I never understood the daddy daughter cliché. I always thought it was cute, but it never totally made sense to me. I could not relate. Everything that she is getting from her dad I did not have as a little girl. I did not have that memory. I do not and never will. The only memories I had were the ones that were shared with me from others and when I visited my father in prison and stories that he shared. During my visits we talked, ate snacks, and played board games. When I was younger it felt as if I was listening to a stranger (my dad) tell me how much he loved me. I remember every time we were getting ready to leave, he would hug and kiss me, and it was the most awkward moment for me, at that time. My Grandmother did everything in her power to make sure I knew him, and I am forever grateful for her love, dedication, and strength. As I think back, I didn't have my dad to tuck me in at night, watch movies with me, take me on dates or discipline me (whatever that would have looked like, because my daughters father discipline is quite cute) run to my every cry (even if it was just for attention), coach me on the sideline, or simply just be my superhero as a little girl. I did not have any of those moments to reflect on in my past. To be blessed and able to watch my daughter and her dad is priceless and heaven-sent.*

*Over the years my relationship with my father developed into something beautiful and my love for him runs deep. He is amazing and our relationship is God filled. I would not trade him for no one in the world. He is my saving grace; this is another chapter later.*

*Through my daddy issues as some may call them, this is a fraction of why I fight so hard. Why I am committed to seeing God's promise through my current relationship. Why I fold but do not break. Why I hold him responsible for both of our hearts. Why I do not give up. Why I love. Why I smile. Why I pray. Why devotion is so important. God shared something about us many years ago and I trust his word. His word is my hope. I thank God for being a witness to their relationship. I thank God for my past. I thank God for my hurt. I thank God I do not selfishly think about myself but for our next generation to do better and make changes. Our actions are their futures. We can never run away from our calling. It will always catch up to us and we must face it.*

*Whatever it is that you are facing, whatever is troubling you, whatever brings you joy, whatever is your why. Do not be afraid to confront and challenge yourself to connect the dots. You owe that to the evolving you. The longer we sweep things under the rug and do not address them, the longer they hurt us and control us. The longer they hurt and control us, the longer we hurt others and continue the cycle.*

*Even over the age of forty-one, shit still runs deep...*

*#justagirltryingtofindherway #illnevergiveup #mytearsaremystrength #thisismystory #becourageous #confrontthatthing #callitout*

❤️*Queesh*

# Stand in Your Truth...

Have you ever experienced being in a deep, passionate conversation with someone that was close to you, and they ended up telling you everything that was on their mind in that moment? This was not one of those sit on top of the hill and watch the sunset type of conversations. It was more in the light of them really standing in their truth about their beliefs and sharing a few things about how they felt about you that potentially or did break you down on the inside. It can go both ways depending on where you stand spiritually. In the flesh we make ourselves a part of their journey and in the spirit, we listen and pray. I am not saying what they said about you 'was the truth' but it was 'their truth' in that moment. Although, it really was all about them but because you are heavenly connected to their future it organically involved you as well. I hope that makes sense in a higher calling. In this moment, all their feelings, challenges, and regrets surfaced. Lucky me to be standing on the receiving end, my oh my, how *it hurt like hell to swallow that pain. All their hurt, fears and possible insecurities poured out on you. I am so sorry, but you do not even realize you were built for this just yet. Everything in your mind came across as if it were meant to hurt and destroy you. The pain was deep.*

*When I had the moment to reflect on everything that transpired, I begin to think about it in a different light. I begin to process everything in a different mindset, I began to reminisce when this conversation took place and how it played out. During this time, I was also discovering a newfound strength through my pain and healing from what was said. I begin to look at what was said from a curious view versus a judgmental view. Let me elaborate if I can... Please keep in mind God was working on and through me during this aha moment... there was no way without him I could have realized this epiphany on my own.*

*There will be certain people that come into your life that you highly respect and love that God will use to test/ push you. There will be opportune moments when they will show their unwarranted behaviors and hand you their ass to kiss on a silver platter. They will tell you everything that is wrong with you and how they think it should be without any remorse for how you feel or how damaging their words can be to you. Not thinking twice about what you will go through to get over the emotional damage it may cause. At least at that very moment in your life, before you matured, that is how it can feel. Almost like the world was f'ing ending. Did you ever stop to think, they might just be standing in THEIR TRUTH and standing firm in what they believe in. Think about that deeply for a minute and try to gain an understanding versus judging them and popping off. As we talk a little more, can we try to remember that our individual journey's will look different from everyone else's and it is especially important for us to steer away from being caught up in the words people say, even though they can be very hurtful. Avoid allowing yourself to get caught up and say things you will regret or do things that take you out of character. Geezzz, I failed this test numerous times. Remember sometimes, hurt people hurt people. You should only take away what you can from the conversation if it adds value to who you are and why you are here. What does not matter, get rid of it. Just toss it. Do not take their problems and make them yours. Hell, your plate is probably already full...*

*I recall various situations while working, being a manager, being a peer, different friendships, and relationships. I wanted to try and help change people to be better and reach the potential I saw in them clear as day. I was checking in on them, challenging them, pushing them, etc. I had to learn that just because God gave me insight that did not mean he assigned that person or their journey to me. I had to learn that everyone is on various levels. When I would take on assignments that were not assigned to me and took matters into my hand my darn ego, I begin to push them beyond their ability and season. Ohhh the seasons... Although I was called to plant seeds which was my only true assignment, God did not tell me to water the seeds. That part. I felt that Holy Spirit.*

*Everything else I was doing was pushing them to break and even possibly resent me or themselves in that breaking moment. I was there so I was the one that ended up receiving the backlash. Hurtful things were said and done. At least that is how I felt. At that moment, at that time in their life, throughout their journey, that was just their truth. Simple as that. Now I find myself thanking them for their truth. Weird, huh? Maybe not when you cross that hurdle. I had to realize that I can only change myself. I had to learn that when people are ready to change, they will change and the effort that is required from me when they seek my guidance will be minimal. It should not require a lot from me but more from them. When they come to me, regardless, if it is good, bad, or indifferent this is the moment I must decipher what is my assignment. What is it that God is asking me to deliver I love this.*

*My friends, this is just my truth and my journey. One thing, regardless of what you think, it took courage for them to say what they said. They thought about it before it came out and even if they did not, they will.*

*We can easily allow our emotions to kick in and take over and it can be a disaster. I know most of you can relate to that internal battle between your natural self and your spiritual self. I thank God that in my later years he has allowed my spiritual self to kick in and keep us aligned, focused and together. Many times, my spiritual self is yelling, "focus Queesh, focus." Then, I ask myself, "what can you learn in this moment from this test?" or "God, what are you teaching me?" "Please make it clear because I don't want to fail." Ask yourself, "are you going to rise and pass the test or are you going to fail?" The choice is yours and this is your test and your journey. I have not aced this test yet, but I am still learning.*

*So, to all my readers take heed to every relationship that you encounter; the good, bad, and indifferent. Grab ahold of the things, people, phrases & actions that give your LIFE excitement (sometimes they make your head snatch back and the old you try to appear into the picture), and at that moment just tell them 'Thank you.'*

*I may have to start a blog because I want to hear some examples of growth moments when you encounter this. I am so excited for us. We are growing and glowing and it looks good on us!*

*Do not forget to reflect...*

*Love Queesh*💗

# The Moment I Stopped Feeling Like a Failure...

People look at me and judge me based on all the materialistic things I have, how I carry myself, my family, and my successful career. Currently, today I make over six figures annually. On the inside, I was or at least thought I was noticeably confident in all areas of my life, and I was not! Many moments I felt like a failure. I often questioned my every move. Doubted myself about what was next and consistently felt empty. This lasted for many years, and it took me a while to snap out of it. Then I slowly begin to wake up! Today, I am so thankful for God breaking me and putting me back together for him. It is taking a lot of soul searching and understanding the word to reach this place in my life.

The moment I stopped feeling like a failure... I begin to do all the things that felt good, that felt right, and organic to me but may have been considered wrong in the eyes of others because it did not align with what was on their agenda.

I started saying yes to me, MORE... And no to the things that I had no interest in doing...

The fear and anxiety begin to slowly leave the more I said yes to the things I thought would upset my family and friends that may make them feel abandoned.

The moment I stop saying yes to things that everyone else benefit from and even though it did not bother me it was not what I necessarily wanted to do, I just went with the flow...

I stopped thinking I failed at being the best mom I could be because I was never married to neither one of my children's fathers.

I stopped thinking I failed my department, team, and peers if I took time off when I needed it for my mind, body, and soul...

I continued to stop focusing on how I feel today knowing that tomorrow would bring on challenges that required a different type of strength to get through... this is still a struggle...

I thought about how I would feel in the future with a clear mind to tackle my problems only to realize it would just be a darn memory.

*I stopped focusing on what everyone else did to me and thought about what they did to themselves. I am a Queen!*

*I embraced saying, "no" with ease.*

*I embraced ME.*

*I begin to love everything about me being imperfect... I was over trying to be perfect because truthfully, it was boring.*

*I started thinking more about having seven streams of income to create generational wealth.*

*I started having daily devotion consistently... Thanking GOD first and giving him all the glory.*

*I stopped being so hard on myself. I gave myself GRACE and UNCONDITIONAL LOVE.*

*I started remembering who the f*ck I was, and it felt amazing... I no longer felt trapped...*

*Be great my loves... Stop doubting yourself... Live for you... Be kind and loooove... I love you!! You got this! We got this... We are not failures! WE were built for this!*

*#Helpmefixmycrown #Letmehelpyoufixyourcrown*

*Queesh*

**Anquesha Tillman**

Never Forget Who The F*ck You Are

# Apologies, Forgiveness and Being Intentional...

Have you ever had someone apologize to you, but you did not ask for their apology? Have you ever apologized but did not mean it, because you knew you were going to do the same thing over again? Maybe you apologized because deep down you did not mean to hurt that person, but you were still trying to figure yourself out. During it all, sometimes it may seem as if they did you a favor by apologizing or maybe you act as if you did them a favor. What if they are not sincere? What if you were not sincere? What do you do with an apology from a person, but their behavior does not change? Why did you apologize if you did not plan to change? What if you find yourself stuck in a pattern with this person or people? What do you do? Does it build resentment over time? Do you continue this behavior because they forgave you so easily? Do you lose respect for yourself? Did they lose *respect for you? Do you begin to judge their character? Are your actions causing them to judge you? Tough subject when you need to look at this through various lenses.*

*I had my share of people apologizing repeatedly in my life but never changed their behavior. Has this every happened to you? I had to be strong enough to decide what I was willing to tolerate in my life. It does not mean I have to stay in their life, and it does not mean I have to go. As I was going through it, I had to decide and move forward on my timing. If you are that person that find yourself apologizing repeatedly for the same reason. Please stop and reflect on your actions and figure out your why. Do not be afraid to dig deep. What are you doing to others? What are you doing to yourself? Place yourself gently in their shoes, how did it make you feel just by thinking about it? Regardless of what end of the stick were on, let's focus on being more intentional with our words and our ways. If we cannot get right for others, we owe it to ourselves, to get right for us. Keep in mind that our expectations for someone else, are just that, our expectations. So, try not to set the bar too high, unfortunately, they will miss our bar because it was never their goal to begin with. All our journeys are SO different and even though our paths will cross from time to time, they will never run parallel to one another. Their battle is not your battle, and your battle is not theirs. We are all fighting to finish this race.*

*We are still learning so much about life and unfortunately, there was no manual created telling us step by step what decisions to make in the flesh. I am starting to realize that no matter what another person's actions are, I must keep striding and learn to forgive for healing to continue to prosper with or without an apology. I must be intentional about MY growth. In the midst of it all, I can only change MYSELF and love others (near or far).*

*We are not here to judge, but sometimes we must face facts or others' beliefs.*

*Love Queesh*❤

# There's a Difference Between Changing on Your Own or Being Forced...

The growth process of changing will look and feel different when you initiate the change and intentionally hold yourself accountable for being a better you... this will be you versus you... instead of you versus someone else telling you how to change or what's best for you, even when you know their advice may be solid... think about this for a second before you move on... be 100% honest with yourself while you're thinking and reflecting on this... a few aha and head-nod moments huh?!?! It is ok, smile... no one knows what took place...

Do you remember turning 18 (or even before that) when you started thinking you could take care of yourself?

*Do you remember the first time you called yourself standing up to your parents? You do not have to share in detail what happened, but do you recall the chapter(s) in your life?*

*How do you feel when someone tells you what you NEED to do? Stay here for a minute... does your ego kick in and immediately say, "aht aht... now wait a minute... You have no clue what I NEED to do..." were you listening to understand what they were saying or listening to respond after you heard the word NEED...*

*Is it harder to take this advice from people that know you and genuinely love you versus people that do not know you and tend to agree with you on various levels? Think about this for a second and stay here until you are ready to move on...*

*It's crazy, right? The things we go through in life trying to find our path. Friends, please remember that when we chat, we want to keep everything transparent and honest with ourselves. Did you ever tell a few people what they need to do? Hello, be real throughout this transformation... I know I told plenty of people... So why when someone tell us what we need to do we get all anxious, mad, and stuck in our feelings... are you laughing at yourself or nodding at the truth, because I am laughing at myself.*

*Do you find yourself getting mad because they were right? Do you find yourself getting mad because they are wrong? Did you find anything positive in the advice they gave you after removing all your emotions and ego? Why did this make us mad in the first place? Is it because we know it is time to level up and leave our childish behaviors behind? Now that is an entire word to reflect on for a minute.*

*Do you think they were looking out for our best interest?*

*When you think back on a time that you decided to do something, was there less resistance because you initiated the change? Was it your power? Was it your drive? Was it ever something that someone else told you before that resonated in you and you felt there was some truth? Did it leave you pondering and festering on the advice?*

*Stay here for a second and think through the difference.*

*So, what did you think as you pondered on your encounters? Did you notice if you were humble and meek, or did you allow your EGO to take over?*

*Regardless of what took place, as you go through the transition it is your choice as to when and how you change...*

*In the end, God will get the glory and some of the people telling us what we need to do could be God sent...*

*Be great... this is not about you... there is a higher calling... I love you... it is time for us to elevate... the kids can teach us too... God uses who he sees fit... you cannot argue with that.*

*Queesh*

# Let Your Guard Down...

*I* know we all recall opening that new chapter or revisiting an old chapter wondering if we will see, hear, or feel something different this time. In our mind, we think THIS damn time, the ending will be different. Maybe I missed a page, could the message be different, did I understand all aspects of this? Did I miss the f'ing assignment? Hell, let me have someone else chime in and provide me with some advice... mommy, sister, brother, friend number 1, 2, and 3... Lawd, I am still stuck... I mean they all hyped me up and it sounded good at the moment but hmmmmm, here we go again, here I go again. I am back to square one, still confused as hell and I just literally jumped right back to it and the only thing that I noted is that my mindset is a little different and I have a slightly different approach. Maybe. My guard is still up, and I am still trying to protect myself from the unknown. When we are in this stage, we must realize that we are not allowing ourselves to be 100% free. We are shortchanging ourselves. We are not being brave. Too often we say to ourselves let's go, we got it this time, THIS TIME is seriously it!

*What I am learning is how to breathe, how to pray, and how to allow my heart to be open and just go with the flow and stop having so many expectations. I am learning to stop holding back when opportunities knock on my door. I am learning to walk through the door. We all get multiple chances at any test and when we do, this in our moment to fulfill ourselves (you will not be able to testify to this until you graduate). Everything is perfectly timed, and you will know clearly when you should turn the last page in that chapter. We are allowing ourselves to be very vulnerable by practicing this and I applaud us for that. There is strength gained and lessons learned throughout the process to carry to the next chapter. Remember to bring everything and all prior experiences with you... Be wiser but not afraid, THAT is the key. The more you hold back the more you keep yourself as a prisoner on the inside and you will never understand or experience the joy of being able to close one chapter and walk away gracefully and meek into the next chapter of your life.*

*Try it and see what happens. I am so excited for you. During this process, remember, do not lose yourself. Remember to Smile, Laugh, Pray, or Sip - but do not judge, now go be great!*

*Love Queesh*💗

# Understanding My Purpose and Loving Myself...

# Defining Success...

Defining success is fun to understand for yourself. Maybe. I chuckled on the inside; life is full of surprises. I encourage you to ask a few people to define success and based on my experience, I think their definition will differ slightly from one person to the next. Do not be afraid to ask individuals with diverse backgrounds so that you have a truly diverse set of answers to expand your mindset. Asking the same people that share your same values, might keep you trapped inside of a box, and 'may' limit your growth. Try to switch it up to expand your norm. It was interesting for me when I did this.

According to webster's definition, success is the accomplishment of an aim or purpose. Marinate on that for a moment before you move on.

When setting your goals and defining success keep in mind this can be measured very differently from person to person... To some it may resemble money, helping others, *having a certain job title, living in a certain neighborhood, meeting your parents or spouse's expectations, or even driving a certain car.... but this is YOUR life so please be comfortable defining it as you see fit for you. There should never be any judgment for how someone else defines THEIR success.*

*Their story is their truth and I love that for everyone. When you decide what success means to you do not be afraid of what others think. Stand firm and believe in yourself. Remember, you were strategically placed.*

*I often ask myself, "what is the most important thing in your life today?" "What can I think of, that bring happiness and fulfillment to me?" If you have the same thoughts that I have, I encourage all of us, including myself to write this down and keep an incredibly open mind as we grow in our experiences and gain exposure. I noticed, this changed for me as time passed me by and I learned to be ok with it. My loves, be ok to change and redefine yourself over and over and over and over until the final product is complete. You were born free.*

*#besuccesful #gradualbabysteps #beawesome #stayfocused #beconsistent #Iloveyou #loveyourself #successstories*

❤Queesh

# Starting Over...

*I* could not ask for a better group of people to discuss 'Starting Over' with because of the journey that we have set forth for ourselves. We have all heard this simple statement more than once in our life... 'Starting Over'... What specifically crossed your mind when you read the title? Did you do a quick head tilt with a smirk? Did it instantly send you down a path you cared not to travel down? Did you begin to feel fear or worry? Did you feel any other emotion just by thinking about really having to start over? If you did, it is natural when you think about starting over, no matter what task is in front of you.

The more I think about this and all I have endured; I have come to the realization that we are never starting over even when it feels as if we are. We are continuing the process of defining who we are and where we are going. Each time this opportunity is presented to me, I think about all the new experiences I have gained from *my prior lessons and oh my do I smile that will inevitably help me navigate through this next chapter. I realized, I had to change my mindset.*

*Throughout life we can become comfortable and complacent out of habit. I know for me; I became busy chasing my career. I worked extremely hard to get where I am today, and the path is still unraveling.... I spent most of my time taking care of my kids and my family no complaints. When we have a moment to rest, we do not really allow ourselves to take an actual BREAK from all the things that consume our time and energy. When we stay in this pattern, we can become stuck. This becomes our everyday life and before we know it a decade or two have passed us by. When we are stuck at a crossroad it can feel like eternity. These moments in life can sometimes make us want to give up and even push it all under the rug to avoid the pain or the thoughts of the unknown. We often think about everything we could lose if we choose to do something different to redefine ourselves.*

*If we make an intentional decision to move forward down this new path after weighing the pros and cons, I want us to remember that starting over may not feel healthy at first but if we focus on our future, that will allow us to move through this next chapter much easier. We know we cannot change the past and truthfully living in the past, wishing, and hoping will only get us that much closer to our death bed with many regrets on chances we never took. The thought of deciding NOT to change when our hearts are beating fast and telling us to jump will haunt us.*

*My friends, do not be afraid to take that leap. The hardest part is deciding to jump. Once you jump, the rest is history. It will not fall into your lap at once but progression over time will reveal your new chapter. YOU will have some work to do (this is key). You will continue to grow (many lessons to be learned are in store for you). You will be required to set goals, but just remember to take all the lessons learned before this one and apply them to who you are today and who you are evolving to become that is your reward.*

*My spirit and soul tell me that one day it will all click. I have been through this process before and I know you have too, so as we continue to navigate through life, get excited about these new chapters that are presented in front of us! Let's get excited even during the pain. What did God say?!*

*Do not forget to reflect and hold yourself accountable, you got this.*

*#fixyourcrowns #don'tworryaboutwhatth eywillthink #stayfocused #staydetermined #knowwhothef*ckyouare #makebigthingshappen #knowyourpurpose #dontcheatonyourself*

*Queesh*

# Understanding Your Purpose...

*D*o you understand why you are still standing after all your trials and tribulations? Do you understand why you are still here even when you feel like you are undeserving? Do you understand why you were given another chance after all your downfalls? Do you understand your purpose? What does having a purpose mean, while we are navigating through life? Do you understand your blueprint? Do you realize what you are capable of accomplishing? Do you understand the impact of your influence? My God.

Please take the time to think and reflect and remind ourselves that we are unique. We were perfectly made and there is no one else like us. There are many times we tend to lose our fire and all we have is smoke lingering and we are confused if we are in danger or out of danger. Many times, we lose our energy because it feels as if we are going in circles. Before we know it, the passion and *energy are gone. Before we find the energy again to keep going strong, it takes something else to drastically happen.*

*Think about that last time someone made you angry or things did not go exactly the way you planned. You found a ton of energy to clean and reorganize. All kind of ideas popped in your head. You were doing well, and nothing could stop you. You just mapped out your life in 2 minutes. You had it all figured out. Did you do this to prove something to someone or did you do this to prove something to yourself? Imagine being on fire like that every day! I am here to tell you, although that energy and vibe will not be like that 100% of the time, we have the power to make it happen. No one on this earth can MAKE us better. They can deposit a seed, but everything is God sent. I DON'T CARE how connected we feel to people. Our blueprint was designed, and our destiny is OUR destiny! What was birthed inside of us has always been there. It is up to each one of us to execute and find our purpose and drive. We did not make it this far without a higher help or something that was built inside of US! Think over your childhood years and all your accomplishments. Losing your first tooth, riding a bike, going skating, etc. Nothing came easy but something inside of YOU pushed through for you to get up and conquer.*

*I want you all to stop what you are doing for 30 seconds and think about that last time you felt like a million dollars. Think about the last time you felt amazing. Do you remember what you did that made you feel that way? Dig deep my friends. Once you remember it, write it down and do more of that (this is your life's best practice). Did you feel that energy rush just thinking about it? Did you chuckle and nod your head? If so, THAT'S IT!!!! Do more of that and be intentional about your moves! We are not doing this to prove ourselves to NO ONE, we are doing this to align with the universe and fulfill our purpose.*

*Always remember loves, you are like no other, there is not another soul exactly like you... Do you have similarities to them? Absolutely, but nothing is the same and just maybe we need to remind ourselves of that each day when we rise... we deserve THAT! OUR blueprint is OURS... We have something that the world needs to see... continue to tap into our greatness and discover it. Only we can conquer this... The best thing about it is that we have the drive and road map on how to reach our destiny... how we affect others... and what legacy we want to leave behind. We drive this by being intentional. We can also choose to do nothing and stay stuck in the same cycle. The choice is ours.*

*My friends, please reflect on how you feel today and follow up in six months and hold yourself accountable for your future. Set a date, set realistic goals, and add a quick reminder to your calendar, and go out there and do important things.*

*#Helpmefixourcrowns #KingsandQueens #YouGotThis #SeasonsAreReal #LoveEverySeason #GainTheLesson #FindYourPurposeBeingIntentional*

❤️*Queesh*

# Trust the Process...

*T*rust the process, trust the process, trust the darn process... ok already, I get it... but wait, what process are we trusting? You understand I am going through a million things right now, right? That is what I am constantly telling myself right now as I keep hearing trust the process... Many times, the process that is right in front of us is not the process that is the ultimate process that we should be focusing on. Tongue twister huh... read that last sentence again. This 'thing' that currently has our attention is just a small section of the puzzle that will not even stand out once our journey is concluded.

Friends... deep sigh and shaking my head... can I just tell you what transpired within me to begin to write this chapter, let me rewind the hands of time.

When I first wrote the title to this chapter it was well before I even knew what I wanted to write but the title

DROPPED in my spirit about 3 weeks before I even began writing... I was aiming to share something else with you all.

I am sitting at Chateau Elan in Braselton, Georgia on July 22nd, 2020, watching the sunset, people, and enjoying a glass of wine!

Pause, the restaurant is about to close in 7 minutes, and I need to get another glass of wine.

Ok, I am back... as I disclosed in another pearl, this is one of the trips I took away to have me time so that I could hear.

So about 3 weeks before writing, the title came to me and dropped 'in my spirit'. When this happens, I always capture the first thought(s) (this is important, so you do not miss your opportunity) and add it to my iPhone or iPad so I do not forget. I told myself I would not focus on meeting a specific deadline for this book and I would just go with the organic flow. I feel like my bestie in this chapter, very long-winded to get to the point, but I wanted to paint and highlight all the moments for you all.

So, I am sitting here, and I am thinking... trust the process... Ok Lord, what are you about to reveal to me? You just keep blowing my mind with the things you continue to show me. Everything that we go through should be used to help others through love and kindness and to share the word and the gospel is becoming my reality. Everything in life we go through is for a bigger reason and that reason is not about us. In this process, I had to remove myself and my voice for God to do HIS work. We can only USE our platform or gift to help others through kindness and love through our walk and by being obedient. I realized I cannot change others! God said, "that is my role... I AM who I AM, the Alpha and the Omega... you are just my help." At that moment, my AHA moment left me full.

I know I cannot finish this chapter today because I just had this epiphany, and I am still going through the process. The first step to this process was a lot of crying, more crying, asking why, worshiping, praying, and did I mention a ton of crying? That also included lack of focus, uncertainty, lack of confidence, asking why, blaming self, not eating, NOT drinking my water (thank you Sister Sarah), and confusion.

Then, there came my reality/perspective while still crying, but hearing clearer, making better sense of things, and understanding that I can never lean on my understanding. I learned through this process that I must trust God (PERIOD), forgive, move forward, put out positive energy, stay determined and value my f'ing worth!

*That is where I am right now... I know there will be more but at this moment my heart found peace and God confirmed he is proud of me. My eyes are filled with happy tears, and this is what is in front of me, a bright future.*

*#Hope #Love #ButGod*

❤️*Queesh*

# *I Dare You to BET on Yourself...*

I dare you to BET on yourself all the time. Bet on yourself and embrace your confidence. Bet on yourself that you are THE chosen one. Bet on yourself that you can conquer whatever you put your mind to. Bet on yourself that when you ignite your passion, dedication, and focus you are destined to survive and thrive. Can you do that for yourself? Do you understand how powerful this transformation will be? Imagine, another servant winning at God's work, and it is you. Can you imagine all of us betting on ourselves to WIN? That is BIG! Bigger than we could ever visualize. Betting on yourself will take accountability for all your actions. This part. Be open and honest with yourself about how you treat people, how you treat yourself, and how you define winning. If you are defining winning based on all your successes, you are possibly looking at this all wrong. Throughout this journey, you will have to remain consistent and honest with yourself, brutally honest. If you cannot do this or you are not prepared, take the time to think *about the commitment that you are about to muster. If your heart is beating fast, take that leap. It does not have to be perfect; God will perfect it over time. It is not an easy journey. Betting on yourself does not mean that you are better than anyone else, so we must remain humble and exhibit kindness throughout this process. You cannot forget these important aspects of this journey. Even if you do, all good, we are blessed with a loving God that will allow us to try again. You will realize that when you are betting on yourself you are also betting on others while helping them reach their goal for the better good. That is an everlasting reward. That is our purpose as it all comes around full circle. Go out and be great!*

*Share this moment with us on a later day, I am so excited about your transformation. I am betting on you, and I am cheering for you!*

*#DontForgetToFollowUpandReflect*

*❤Queesh*

# Ponder on This...

When you answer these questions be very transparent and honest with yourself. Do not just stop at the first thing that comes to mind. Dig deep. Being honest with yourself will help you reach your next level. Become who you are called to be.

Do you understand your strengths and how to value them?

Do you understand your weaknesses and how to value them?

Do you understand your role and responsibilities?

Do you often play the victim or accept responsibility for your behavior?

Do you hold yourself accountable?

What do you have to offer to the universe?

What are your core principles in life?

*Do you believe in giving grace to yourself and others?*

*Who are you?*

*Take the time to reflect on your answers and visit this again to see where you stand.*

*Keep Glowing & Growing.*

*❤Queesh*

# Stop Procrastinating...

Ugggggghhhhhh, procrastination!!

My oh my, as I roll my eyes. Procrastination embodies everything that keeps us from being great. It robs us of our desires, goals, passion, love, time, dedication and so much more. DO YOU UNDERSTAND WHAT I AM SAYING, FRIENDS?

Think about the last time you were ready to make something happen, you had a plan, you were ready, you were excited, and then BOOM!!! Before you know it, you were doing everything under the sun that kept you from reaching the goal you intended to crush and felt wholeheartedly to fulfill. Then you begin to make excuses for the one thing that was sooooo important to you just an hour ago. Suddenly, the flame to your fire is dead... POOF says the magic dragon, it's gone just like that. The excuses that you just created in your mind, REALLY?! Take a second and really think about all the excuses *that you made on why you can postpone this project until next week. LOL, as you roll your eyes at yourself and laugh because you know it is true, right? That ish makes no sense at all, your reason that you told yourself today or yesterday is garbage. So, why do we do that to ourselves repeatedly? We deserve better than that. Treat yourself like the King or Queen that you are and commit to finishing what you started without adding Mr. or Ms. Procrastination to the mix.*

*You see where I am going with this topic of discussion at hand. Our number of days on earth is limited and if we do not fulfill our destiny that is aligned to our BLUEPRINT, then what are we needed for? What are we here for? Everyone was created with a special gift before being created in our mother's womb. So, if God went to the extreme of giving this special gift to you AND it was/is free, original, and authentic, why not take advantage of fulfilling this. Someone once reminded me that I only have 1,440 minutes in a day, so BE PRODUCTIVE my loves.*

*If you do not make it happen, no one else can because your GIFT is YOUR GIFT!*

*Got it! I love you, now go be GREAT!*

*Queesh*

# Selfish or Not...

$S$peaking from experience... Many times, as a woman or a mother we always put our families first... I'm not saying it's negative, but I want to share my truth for a second... Honestly, when you think about it, we (as women) were made this way, and it's part of our design. I embrace the love and nurturing that I have to support my family, and I love every aspect of it. Raising children does not stop when they turn eighteen. Managing does not stop at 5 pm. Did you ever realize that the bills never take a breaks, the house messes itself up, and groceries are gone on the day you buy them. Illness creeps in whenever it wishes and teachers assign more work for the kids to complete at home versus in school. Significant others need attention, friends want to hang out and family members need you as well. Oh, and never forget about the fur babies with four legs. During all of this and at the end of the day I find myself exhausted and end up neglecting myself from the things I need to refuel myself.

*That includes my dreams, aspirations, health, body, soul, spirit, and mind. People often tell me that I make it look easy. It is not that I do not take care of myself or search for what truly sparks my fire but oftentimes I neglect the young lady inside that would love to live, breathe, and be in the moment before that moment passes me by. The trapped lady inside would like to just escape for a few minutes throughout the day, just to scream and be free.*

*I used to watch what I say around the kids, watch what I wear, and make sure that I am the epitome of what I think I should be for them and the perfect fit for our family. I created this illusion, and the reality is, they could care less.*

*Just for today and even after today if you feel like it... be you from deep down inside and just live. Put on that edgy outfit, wear your makeup how you want to, dance like no one is watching, say whatever you feel like saying (be nice), you don't have to cook or clean (they will be ok), binge watch your shows, take a drive alone and if you don't feel like going home... DON'T!!!! Laugh as hard as you want. Throw away all those long gowns and sleep in what you want to sleep in. If you prefer to be naked, DO IT, the kids should knock first and wait until you say, "come in." If they walk in on you, oh well, I guarantee they will not do it again... you do not have to lock the door if you choose not to.*

*Doing just this will help you be a better version of yourself. Smile, Laugh, Pray or Sip... Just do not judge ❤ I love you ladies and love the men that support this!*

# The Assignment or Not...

Did you realize as you were navigating through that last moment of frustration the issue you wanted to resolve was not your assignment? Well, that is what I ended up telling myself... As a mother, daughter, sister, friend, cousin, co-worker, neighbor, etc. I found myself assigned and attached to everyone's challenges. As soon as I meet someone and get to know them more on a personal level, I desire to push them to reach whatever goal they were or were not aiming for. I wanted to protect them from the destruction I was seeing Jesus help me. I was walking around like little Ms. F'ing Fix-it. Let me explain, typically individuals share their personal life with me, seeking advice, needing a shoulder to lean on, or confiding in me to be a sounding board. I immediately feel responsible and connected to whatever they were trying to sort out. While looking and listening to them, I can see so much potential forming on the inside waiting to be birthed. I could even see this in the worst situations. My mind is *always optimistic, so I wanted to help, I was yearning to help, I was always thinking how I can help while praying or better yet asking the Lord to please use me. I would find myself stuck sometimes but would continue asking over and over like a toddler, how can I serve you, God, in this situation.*

*As I grew spiritually, I begin to easily see the good in all people. This is what the Bible teaches us, it teaches us to love and to be kind, and to help when people are in need. At first, I did not always love, like, or understand this about my journey but I grew to fall more in love with it as I began to understand who I was becoming, at least that is what I thought. Everyone that I encountered, I wanted to see them bloom into the true potential butterfly they could be. I was the one seeing all this right before my eyes. I could see the transformation and it was always beautiful. I had to realize that if they cannot see, feel, or visualize it, they would never totally hear anything until they were ready. Not from me, not from anyone. Our thoughts would never align no matter how hard I pushed and believed in them. I had to learn that everyone has their journey and God's timing is perfect. I had to understand this was my gift and not theirs. I developed a sense of trying to help people without them even asking for my help or guidance in some cases. In my world, in my mind,*

*I just wanted to help them see what I saw in them with a burning passion. Overtime my expectations of others brought on many disappointments that lead to heartbreaks and it left me feeling burned out. I would be disappointed when things did not click or line up for the individuals the way I saw fit for them. The more I dedicated time to my devotion and quiet time I finally had an aha moment that although my heart wanted the best for everyone that I interacted with, all assignments DID NOT belong to me. Most of them was never for me to take on outside of being kind and showing love. Wow Queesh, this was NOT your assignment, now that is a full word. God was not calling me to see everything through from A to Z for everyone and overexert myself. Yes, while he allowed our paths to cross, he never said I am assigning this task to you, my child. I had to step back and ask myself, who was I fooling. Why did I think I was capable to save all these people? At the end of the day, all of them were NOT assigned to me. I know you are thinking but it got you here and yes, you are right it did and that is exactly why I am sharing this with you all, but it still was not all assigned to me. I realized I was carrying too much on my shoulders that was never meant for me to carry. I had to learn that it was not my role, my responsibility, or my journey. When I had this aha moment within myself, within in my life, it was a very awakening moment for me to understand that I could still be me and walk through my journey and my calling without carrying what felt like the world on my shoulders and live free. I did not realize all this time, that some of it was my pretty little ego. My ego wanted to take on the world. I was confused but excited every time I met someone new. I always thought yay, I got you God. I want to be the best servant I can be! I realized that everyone's journey is designed just for them and although our paths will cross at some point for a minute, second, season, or lifetime I may never truly know the outcome of their story. I was only destined to be there for that moment and during my time I was only supposed to allow my light/life to shine through with love and kindness. Although, I would love to see each of them glow and grow, the glory is not for me but for our God. I learned that as people go through their journeys, they will eventually figure it all out just the way God ordained them to. It is not meant for me to be assigned to everyone that crosses my path but for me to live my life as it is designed for me. My walk will be my testimony and light for others. May God keep us all wrapped in his arms for protection, love, guidance, and peace. What is meant to be will be. We have the power to excel as he is our source! We can only be the ultimate change in our lives as he works in and through us that we desire to see, no one else. No one else can take credit for his work. Realizing that I had an ego and it had to die for me to live was life changing.*

*My friends when I say I love you... I mean it, but I had to remove some weight to live free... I will continue to love, support, and be kind but I will only take on what God assigns to me!*

*❤JustQueesh #Anquesha #LaShawn #Tillman #40 #EgoUCantLiveHere*

# Dear Me in my 30's...

*Dear me in my 30's,*

*I am so proud of the woman that you embodied for three thousand, six hundred, and fifty full days. You embraced and conquered everything that was placed in your path. You stood with dignity and grace. You pushed through adversity and never backed down from a challenge. You took on most tasks that many people said, 'oh hell nawwww' too. You sacrificed many moments of yourself for others. You were gracefully broken and strategically put back together. You discovered so many different seasons and accepted them for what they were in that moment. Your career took off, you gave birth to a beautiful baby girl, you sold your 1st purchased home, you bought a bigger home for your babies, you lost loved ones, you traveled with no regrets, you fell in love with Jamaica, your saving accounts are on point, you learned to love unconditionally, you made some wrong decisions, your relationship with God grew deeper, your firstborn graduated from High School and College, you bought cars as you wanted, you invested and believed in people and your mindset continued to shift year after year. You cried a lot, you were depressed a lot, you were happy a lot, you were confused a lot, you battled with yourself a lot, at times you did not know your self-worth, but still, you stood strong, and you were not a force to be f'd with. You gave a lot, but you also took more bullshit than you should have. You continued to network and educate yourself and others. You started understanding your purpose better which led to understanding and loving people deeper. You started putting things into perspective. You started to realize what mattered and what did not matter. You started rebuilding old relationships. You continued to tap into your purpose. For all that you endured, I am here to let you know how proud I am of you. Not because of all the 'things' you acquired but for your strength and tenacity to stay the course. I love you because you saw and felt our vision and purpose and understood the big picture. I love you because you understood that this is all bigger than just us! I love you because without your challenging work ethic, your sacrifice, your dedication, your faith, and your unwavering love I would NOT be the woman that I am today! So, Anquesha LaShawn Tilman,* between the ages of thirty — thirty-nine, lady I am PROUD of YOU! I pray that all you have deposited into us, I can get us through this next decade.

You were BRAVE and I can see your footprints #❤️🥂 #JustQueesh

# Never Forget
## who the F*ck you are

This one resonated in my soul from the time I was in my twenties through my entire thirties and now as a constant reminder in my forties. I always found myself wishing that I knew what I know today, years earlier. When I put things into perspective the timing is always perfect according to how and when it should be aligned with what I was facing during that part of my journey. There were moments in my life that I questioned, who am I? Where am I going? What is my purpose? What should I do next? Where do I get advice? Who should I follow, who should I listen to, and how to understand what matters? After I bounced these questions around in my head, I started asking myself how much longer will I ask these questions? Is anyone else feeling the pain or having confusion like I am? Where and when will my breakthrough come through? I begin thinking, this *growth does not feel organic. This is not me. Is all this worth it? Should I revert to my old ways? I should not be changing my authenticity through it all, so why do I feel like I am? Then I begin thinking, I feel like I am losing myself, but during it all, I did not realize it is my growth and breakthrough moment throughout my journey and I cannot stop now. No matter what I am faced against, I have to keep going.*

*Many times, throughout my journey, I asked God, "why me?" I asked, continuously, "Lord why me." His answer was always, why not you, my child? I uncovered that I must continue to challenge myself when that question arises in my mind that always make me second guess the ability of God to work through me and my testimonies.*

*My friends, wisdom is REAL, and I am so happy that as I age and experience life my wisdom and yours develops into something magical that will continue to mold me for what my future holds. Eventually, I will be able to answer most of the questions I ask myself, maybe. Throughout this journey, I will continue to learn more about myself than I could ever imagine.*

*If you are willing to take the ride, put your seatbelt on and go with the flow. I am not saying it will be easy and I am not saying it will be uneventful but let's make a promise to ourselves that we will remain focused on our* calling that brings glory to our savior. Bringing change was never meant to happen overnight. I honestly believe that we all have a purpose, but all are called differently. As we are going through our journey, make it the best experience that we will ever accomplish. We will be so thankful for every sleepless night, the moments we wanted to give up, and the moments we wanted to punch the next person that yelled out, "good morning" or "God is good." Each moment will define every step that was needed for us to reach where we stand today.

I know that while going through the motions we constantly feel the pull of aggravation, but for the sake of yourself in 5 years, be easy on yourself. Show yourself some grace and love. I promise we will thank the younger version of ourselves for being so resilient. REMEMBER we are HUMAN. We were designed to jack things up and we are already given multiple chances to refocus and get it right. My downfall out of all of this was trying to be perfect for everyone around me. Yeah, THAT was MY downfall. During that, I lost who I was. I forgot what I WANTED and found myself on an emotional roller coaster. I forgot WHAT I was called to do and WHO I was called to serve, I was caught up in the fast lane of career projection, being a great mother, etc., etc. I still remember one of my Georgia mothers said, 'don't get caught up,' remember *why you are here. That stuck with me for over 14 years. When I finally pulled myself together, I realized being perfect was BORING AF! When that light bulb hit me, I rededicated MYSELF to MYSELF and said, "never again will I ever forget who the F👑ck I am. That is my truth and my promise. I had to understand within myself that I am cut different, and I am unique, so do not try to figure me out because sometimes I cannot figure myself out. I do not always play by the rules. I go against the grain and will always challenge the status quo. All things that we typically do or learn throughout life are from people that we interact with or people/things we have researched. It does not make them right all the time or a perfect fit for you. So, it is ok for us to be in our lane and 'look' and 'do' things differently. It is time we seek our path and create our own lane. Be ok with thinking differently. I am not saying that my way is right, but this is my truth and my journey. So, while you are going through YOUR journey REMEMBER why you are here and what you are called to do, remember who you serve, and what your purpose is to fulfill. Never Forget Who the F👑ck You Are!*

*Love, Queesh*💗

*#bebad #bebrave #bekind #helpothers #beyou #neverforgetwhoyouare #reflectandprosper*

# About the Author ♥

I started journaling and focused on capturing my emotions and how I felt going through various tribulations many years ago. The more I embraced it, the more I realized I had to capture my thoughts in that moment for them to resonate and be profound enough to share. If I did not, I do not think I could have produced the same energy later.

The year I started this journey was in 2015 when my Aunt Doris fell sick. My auntie was like a fourth grandmother to me. I remember being on a plane and that small but loud voice spoke to me and said, 'write.'

Let us rewind the hands of time for a second. Over 11 years ago, I transitioned from an individual contributor at work to a manager. During this transition I was pregnant with my baby girl, Kourtnie and completed my bachelor's degree program a year prior. At that time, my boys, Juquan and Jaiden, were 12 and 9. Managing people came with more written communication and being professional more than I wanted at that moment in my life. In the beginning, just say I hated every moment of my transition. I was forced to change before I was mentally ready. I could no longer shorthand my communication and speak freely. All I could do was smile when I thought about speaking freely. Everything had to be clear, concise, and professional. Every year in my performance evaluation review, my manager would write, "be careful with your possessive plurals." Each year until it became clear to me, I would always say to myself, "forget those possessive plurals, hunni, this is me!" Today, I get it. Thank you, LT!

When I began drafting this book, all my experiences helped shape my thought process on countless opportunities throughout my life that I wanted to share with you. This is my truth and my story, and I am hoping that someone can take something away and help them thrive in a very unorthodox world.

As you read this, I hope (because hope is needed to find faith or whatever you believe in) that you can clear your mind and find love within yourself to Smile, Laugh, Pray, or Sip but steer away from judging yourself and others. Embrace being nice to ourselves, simply spread love and take yourself out of that box. Be great. Be who God called you to be and never forget that you are a King or Queen!

Love truly wins, love Queesh 

www.ingramcontent.com/pod-product-compliance
Lightning Source LLC
Chambersburg PA
CBHW061136160726
48006CB00038B/2110